HOW TO START YOUR OWN PODCAST

A Step-by-Step Guide to Launching a Successful Podcast

Ray Goodwin

CONTENTS

LIABILITY DISCLAIMER

The information contained within this book is intended for informational purposes only and should not be construed as legal or professional advice. The authors and publishers of this book are not responsible for any losses or damages that may arise from the use of the information contained within.

The reader assumes full responsibility for any decisions made based on the information in this book. The authors and publishers do not endorse any particular method, service or product mentioned in this book and are not responsible for any consequences resulting from their use.

The reader should exercise caution and discretion when making life changing decisions, and should be aware of the risks and potential consequences of their actions. This book is not a substitute for professional or legal advice and should not be relied upon as such.

By reading and using the information in this book, the reader acknowledges and agrees to hold harmless the authors, publishers, and any other parties involved in the creation or distribution of this book from any and all liability, claims, damages, or losses that may arise from their use of the information contained herein.

CHAPTER 1:
INTRODUCTION

Welcome to "How To Start Your Own Podcast"! If you're reading this, chances are that you are interested in creating your own podcast. Maybe you have some great ideas for content, but don't know where to start. Or perhaps you've started a podcast already but feel like it's not reaching its full potential.

Regardless of your situation, I'm here to help guide you through the process of creating a successful podcast from scratch. As someone who has been involved in online sales for over 25 years, I understand the importance of having a strong online presence and how podcasts can be an incredibly effective tool for building a loyal audience.

Throughout this book, I will cover everything from the basics of choosing your topic and format, to recording and editing your episodes, to promoting your podcast through various channels. My goal is to provide you with all the knowledge and resources necessary to produce high-quality content that resonates with listeners and keeps them coming back for more. So let's dive into the exciting world of podcasting together!

Overview

Podcasting is a niche medium that is rapidly growing. It is a digital platform on which you can broadcast a variety of content such as talk shows, interviews, performances, and other audio content on the internet. Podcasts are becoming increasingly popular in today's fast-paced world. They allow people to consume content on the go, during their commutes or workouts, and while they go about their daily business.

This book is designed to help you start your own podcast from scratch. Whether you're a business looking to increase your reach or a hobbyist looking to start a podcasting career, this book will provide you with tools and knowledge to help you get started.

Why podcasting is important?

Podcasting has seen a surge in popularity, and there are many reasons why. For starters, podcasting is a platform with low entry costs and a large audience reach. They are a great way to share your knowledge with a large audience, and they give you the flexibility to create content in your own style at your own pace.

Podcasts also offer a huge variety of audio content, providing listeners with an unparalleled array of options to learn or be entertained. They are easily accessible on most devices, making it easy for listeners to consume content on the go without taking up much time in their busy lives.

Brief history of podcasting

Podcasting has come a long way since its inception. The term 'podcast' was first coined in 2004 by Ben Hammersley in a newspaper article. However, the concept of podcasting originated much earlier when Adam Curry, a former MTV VJ, and Dave Winer, a software developer, created a system to distribute internet radio-style shows in 2000.

Initially, podcasting was not very popular, but the trend began to take off in 2004 with the launch of Apple's iTunes. Apple was the major catalyst for podcasting's growth, as they made it easy for podcasters to create, upload, and share their content with their audience.

Benefits of starting a podcast

There are many benefits of starting a podcast. Podcasts offer a unique opportunity for businesses, individuals, or groups to create and distribute their content to a global audience with low overhead costs. Likewise, podcasts provide an authentic way for listeners to connect with a brand, individual or topic they are interested in.

Running a podcast can also develop a long-term relationship with a listener. Podcasts are an intimate medium and listeners often feel connected to the host or the topic of discussion. This can lead to a meaningful and strong bond of trust between the audience and the podcaster.

Target audience for the book

This book is designed for anyone interested in creating and launching their own podcast, whether as a hobby or for business purposes. It is designed to provide the skills needed to get started and create high-quality podcasts. The book is written in a conversational style, making it accessible to anyone interested in learning about podcasting without any prior experience.

Understanding the basics of podcasting

Podcasting is a digital broadcasting platform for audio content that can be accessed for free by anyone with an internet connection. It offers users an opportunity to create a radio show or an audio file to distribute their content to a wide audience.

Podcasts can be consumed on a variety of platforms, including smartphones, tablets, laptops, and desktop computers. There are many podcasting apps to choose from, including Apple Podcasts, Google Podcasts, Spotify, SoundCloud, and more.

Setting realistic goals for your podcast

Before you start a podcast, it's important to set realistic goals. It enables you to measure your progress and helps you plan ahead. Start by asking yourself the following questions:

- ➤ Why do you want to start a podcast?
- ➤ Who is your target audience?
- ➤ What is your niche?
- ➤ What is your podcasting experience level?
- ➤ How often do you plan to release episodes?
- ➤ What are your preferred metrics for measuring success?

Establishing your niche

One of the keys to a successful podcast is having a clear and defined niche. The niche is the specific area of interest or expertise that your podcast will focus on. By having a niche, you will be able to attract an audience who is interested in your content and give them a specific reason why they need to listen to your podcast.

To establish your niche, consider the following:

- ➤ What is your expertise or passion?
- ➤ Who is your target audience?
- ➤ What are their interests and pain points?
- ➤ What is missing from existing podcasts in your niche?
- ➤ What is your unique angle or approach?

Conclusion

Whether you're starting a new business or looking for a new hobby, podcasting is an excellent way to share your passions and expertise with the world. It is not an orthodox way to build audience and drive your brand. Podcasting is the most consumer-friendly, affordable, and creative platform for every genre and niche field.

With this book, you will learn how to create a high-quality podcast, develop interesting content, and promote it to your target audience. This book is designed to make podcasting accessible to everyone, regardless of prior experience. It will help you take your podcasting game to the next level and make a difference in people's lives.

CHAPTER 2: DEFINING YOUR PODCAST

If you're considering starting your own podcast, it's important to define what your podcast is going to be about and what sets it apart from other podcasts. In this chapter, we will discuss the steps you need to take in order to find your niche, develop a concept, and identify your target audience.

Finding The Right Topic

The topic of your podcast will be the foundation of your show, so it's important to choose something you're passionate about. Take some time to brainstorm and think of topics that interest you and that you believe your target audience would enjoy listening to. If you're struggling, try to think about the things you're knowledgeable and passionate about. These are often the topics that will resonate with your listeners the most.

Choosing A Name

The name of your podcast is important because it's what people will remember your show by. It's important to choose a name that's catchy, memorable and unique. You want to choose a name that tells people what your podcast is about, but at the same time, one that will grab their attention. Keep in mind that simple is always better, and you don't want your name to be too long or complicated.

Establishing Your Brand

Your brand is your podcast's identity and includes elements such as your logo, intro/outro music, graphics, and tone of voice. All of these factors will contribute to the overall impression your listeners have of your show. When creating your brand, it's important to consider what distinguishes your show from others in your niche. What values do you want to convey through your brand? How do you want your listeners to perceive your show?

Developing A Concept

Your concept is what will set your podcast apart from others in your niche. It's what will make your show unique, engaging, and interesting. To develop your concept, consider what specific angle you can take on your chosen topic. Think about what sets your podcast apart from others in your niche and how you can deliver your message in a way that is both informative and entertaining.

Identifying Your Target Audience

Your target audience is the group of people who will be most interested in your podcast. To identify your audience, ask yourself these questions: Who are they? What are their interests? What are their needs and desires? By understanding your target audience, you can create content that will resonate with them and engage them.

Looking At Existing Podcasts For Inspiration

Before you get started, take some time to listen to other podcasts in your niche. This will give you an idea of what works and what doesn't. Take note of the things you like and don't like and think about how you can use this information to create a unique and engaging show.

Conducting Market Research

Market research is an important step in identifying your target audience and developing your concept. You can start by looking at what's already out there in your niche. Consider the types of content that are popular, as well as the topics and themes that are being covered. This will give you an idea of what people are interested in and what gaps exist in the market.

Creating A Unique Selling Proposition

A Unique Selling Proposition (USP) is what makes your podcast stand out from others in your niche. It's what sets your show apart and makes it special. Your USP should be clear, concise, and easy to understand. It should be something that resonates with your target audience and makes them want to listen to your show.

In Conclusion

Defining your podcast is a crucial step in the process of starting your own podcast. By finding the right topic, developing a concept, and identifying your target audience, you can create a unique and engaging show that resonates with listeners. By taking the time to establish your brand and USP, your podcast can stand out from the competition and attract a loyal following.

CHAPTER 3: EQUIPMENT & SOFTWARE

One of the most important aspects of starting a successful podcast is having the right equipment and software. In this chapter, we will discuss the essential gear and tools needed to get started, the best options available, and budget considerations to keep in mind.

Selecting the right microphone:

The microphone is the heart of your podcasting setup, and selecting the right one is essential in ensuring that your recordings sound great. There are three types of microphones: dynamic, condenser, and ribbon. Dynamic microphones are ideal for recording in noisy environments, while condenser microphones are more sensitive and produce a richer sound. Ribbon microphones are the least common and often the most expensive.

When it comes to selecting a microphone, the Blue Yeti and Audio-Technica AT2020 are two popular options. The Blue Yeti is a versatile USB microphone that can be used for a range of recording needs, while the AT2020 is a professional cardioid condenser microphone that is great for voice recording. Both of these microphones provide excellent audio quality and are reasonably priced.

Choosing a mixer (if required):

A mixer is not required for all podcasts and can significantly raise the price of your setup. However, if you have multiple microphones or want to include sound effects and music, a mixer can be useful. Mixers range in price from a few hundred dollars to several thousand dollars, depending on their features and complexity.

Recording software options:

There are many software options available for recording your podcast. Some of the most popular include Audacity, Adobe Audition, and GarageBand. All three of these options are easy to use and provide excellent audio quality. Audacity is a free and open-source option for both Windows and Mac operating systems, while Adobe Audition is a powerful paid option that is perfect for professional podcast production. GarageBand comes premade with all Mac computers and is an intuitive option for beginners.

Editing software options:

Editing your podcast is a critical step in ensuring that your final product is polished and professional. There are many options available for editing software, including Audacity and Adobe Audition, which can be used for both recording and editing.

Other popular options include Hindenburg Journalist and Logic Pro X. Hindenburg Journalist is a paid option that is designed specifically for podcasters and is known for its intuitive interface and excellent audio restoration tools. Logic Pro X is also a paid option that offers a range of professional features, including MIDI support and plugin compatibility.

Online hosting platforms:

An online hosting platform is where your podcast will be stored and distributed to various podcast directories, such as iTunes and Spotify. There are many hosting platforms available, including Libsyn, Podbean, and Buzzsprout. Some of these platforms, such as Libsyn, provide powerful analytics tools to help track your podcast's success.

Headphones and speakers:

When recording and editing your podcast, it's crucial to hear every detail of your audio. Investing in a good pair of headphones and speakers can help you pick up on subtle nuances that might have otherwise gone unnoticed.

Some popular headphone options include the Sennheiser HD280 Pro and the Audio-Technica ATH-M50x. Both options provide excellent audio quality and are affordable. When it comes to speakers, the KRK Rokit 5 G4 and JBL Professional LSR305 offer a great balance of price and quality.

Room acoustics and soundproofing:

Achieving good room acoustics is essential for achieving professional sound quality. Properly soundproofing your recording environment can help eliminate background noise and echo. If you're recording in a small room, consider using foam panels, acoustic blankets, or a portable vocal booth. If you're on a budget, you can also use common household items like rugs and curtains to absorb sound.

Budget considerations:

Podcasting can be an expensive hobby, but there are ways to keep costs down. When selecting equipment and software, focus on what you need rather than what you want. You don't need the most expensive equipment to produce a high-quality podcast.

Consider investing in one or two key items, such as a quality microphone or headphones, and build up your setup over time. You can also search for used gear or less expensive alternatives to help keep costs down.

In Conclusion:

Selecting the right equipment and software is a critical step in setting up your podcasting studio. By focusing on your budget and being strategic about your purchases, you can create a professional-sounding podcast without breaking the bank. Remember to research your options carefully, invest in quality where necessary, and always prioritize the needs of your podcast and its audience.

CHAPTER 4: PLANNING YOUR SHOW

Planning your podcast episodes is crucial to delivering high-quality, engaging content to your audience. It ensures that your show flows smoothly, provides value to your listeners, and helps you meet your goals. In this chapter, we'll cover the essential steps in planning your show - from creating a content calendar to scripting your episodes to preparing for special events.

Scripting Your Episodes

Many podcasters follow a loose script or outline to ensure they cover all the key points in their episodes. This approach provides structure and ensures that you don't forget essential topics or stray from the core message. While some podcasters may choose to wing it, scripting or outlining will help you stay focused and provide a better listening experience for your audience.

When scripting your episodes, be mindful of the following:

❖ Start with a working title for your episode. This helps focus your ideas and gives you a clear direction for outlining your content.

❖ Use bullet points or a list to organise your ideas and ensure you cover everything you want to communicate. Make sure to include the key points you wish to communicate.

❖ If you have guests on your show, consider sending them the outline ahead of time so they know what to expect and can offer feedback or provide additional insights.

❖ Keep your language simple and engaging. A conversational tone is best. You don't want to lose your audience in the jargon, so make sure to simplify where possible.

❖ Include calls to action in your script to incentivise your audience to take action after listening to the podcast.

❖ Make sure your script is concise and you don't include length topics that are not adding value to the podcast.

Creating an Episode Outline

After scripting, the next step is to create an outline for your episode. The outline lists the different parts of the episode - introduction, main content, and conclusion - and summarises what you will discuss during each of these segments.

Here are some key areas to consider when creating your episode outline:

❖ Introduction: This part sets the tone for your podcast, gives a brief overview of the episode, and introduces the listeners to what they can expect.

❖ Main content: This is where the core of your podcast belongs. Here you can focus for longer periods around one central idea or topic. This also includes additional features like guest interviews and sound bites. Ideally, this should take up the bulk of your episode.

❖ Conclusion: This part should summarise the key takeaways from your podcast, including any calls to action, and should provide a clear sense of resolution for your listeners.

Building a Content Calendar

A content calendar is a tool that helps you plan your episodes in advance. It outlines the topics that you will cover in each upcoming episode, includes a timeline for each episode's development, and ensures that you stay on track with your goals.

Consider the following elements when building your content calendar:

❖ Identify the optimal publishing cadence. Depending on audience preferences, the optimal publishing cadence may vary. Some weekly podcasts may find success by releasing their episodes on Thursdays or Fridays, while others might thrive releasing every other week or even monthly.

❖ Plan by season or by topic. You can organise your content around a theme, or you can choose to structure your episodes into a series. Dividing your content into seasons allows you to take a break between runs to plan your next content series and re-energise.

❖ Assign deadlines for various stages and share with your team. Deadlines help keep the content development process on track and ensure that your episodes are produced in time for publishing.

❖ Be flexible in responding to changes in the audience requirements or other external factors. Be open to deviating from your content schedule if new material emerges or current events demand an impromptu episode.

Preparing for Special Events or Promotions

A well-planned special event or promotional episode can give your listeners something unique to look forward to. Similarly, it can serve as an opportunity to generate interest in the podcast, build engagement among your audience, and increase downloads or subscribers.

Consider the below tips when preparing for special events or promotions:

- ❖ Plan well in advance. Give yourself enough time to develop the content, design the marketing materials, and build anticipation in the lead-up to the special event.

- ❖ Think outside the box. Don't be afraid to consider creative event ideas that your audience will find exciting.

- ❖ Be clear and specific. Your promotional episode must have a clear message that the audience understands. It should allow your listeners to understand what they stand to gain from engaging with your brand.

- ❖ Cross-promote across all your media. Spread the word about your special event on your social media platforms, email newsletter or blog and make sure to mention it in previous and upcoming episodes.

- ❖ Leverage the collective strength of your podcast team. Make sure to delegate responsibilities to the members of your team which may include production coordination, concept development, marketing and audience engagement.

- ❖ Plan post-event activities. After the event, make sure to thank attendees or participants, and consider publishing special photos, audio recordings or videos associated with the event on your podcast platform or social media.

Optimising for Search Engines

To ensure that podcast episodes reach a larger audience, podcasters must also optimise their shows for search engines. This involves several strategies, including using the right keywords, optimising your show descriptions and tags, and leveraging social media to gain a broader audience.

Consider the following tips when optimising your podcast for search engine visibility:

❖ Use keyword-rich titles and episode descriptions. Podcast search engine algorithms favour content that includes well-placed and targeted keywords in the titles and episode descriptions that reflect the content of the episode.

❖ Include targeted tags. Include specific tags and keywords around the topics discussed in the episode. This will make it easier for listeners to find your content when searching for similar podcasts.

❖ Provide transcripts. Adding transcripts of your podcast can enhance accessibility by making the information available for those with hearing impairments. Additionally, it boosts search engine optimisation by adding transcripts to your website where search engines crawling it can index and rank the content.

❖ Leverage social media platforms. Marketing your podcasts via social media helps increase your visibility and broadcast it to a greater audience, which in turn improves the listener base.

Conclusion

Planning your show is a critical component of building a successful podcast. By scripting your episodes, creating an episode outline, building a content calendar, and planning for special events or promotions, you ensure that you deliver value to your listeners and stay on track with your goals. Optimising your podcasts for search engines will also serve to increase visibility for your show. With these planning and optimisation strategies, you can take your podcast to the next level and capture a wider audience.

CHAPTER 5: RECORDING

Recording your podcast is where the magic happens. It's the most exciting and creative part of the process, but it can also be the most challenging. A lot depends on getting the technical details right, along with making sure you conduct your interviews in a personable and engaging manner. In this chapter, we'll go through the recording process step by step, so you can create the best possible audio content for your podcast.

Setting up your recording studio:

Before you hit record, you need to make sure you have all your kit set up and that your studio is ready for action. Make sure you've got a quiet space to record in that's free from background noise, with no echo or reverberation. You might want to use sound-absorbing materials to improve your sound quality. There are many options to choose from, including foam tiles, curtains, and in extreme cases, moving blankets.

When it comes to equipment, you'll need:

❖ A quality microphone: Your microphone is the most important part of your set up, they are different types of microphones to choose from, so it's a good idea to research them first. Some of the most popular types include condenser and dynamic microphones. Condensers capture more details and are perfect for environments with no background noise while dynamic microphones are ideal for situations where there is noise in the background.

❖ Headphones: Your headphones will help you monitor your audio levels and ensure that you're not getting any feedback or echo. Get headphones that are comfortable and offer good isolation.

❖ Recording software: There are many options from free to professional software available. Popular choices include Audacity and Reaper.

❖ Recording devices: Use a desktop or laptop to run your recording software or a digital recording device. Ensure the device you are using has enough memory and is compatible with your chosen recording software.

Best practices for recording:

❖ Speak clearly and directly to the microphone: Make sure you're speaking into the microphone and not away from it. Keep a steady pace while speaking and avoid noise or shaking the microphone/headset cord while recording.

❖ Keep things professional: You always want to make sure your guests or co-hosts feel at ease, but don't get overly casual when talking to them during interviews. Remember that any recording or interaction could be used in your podcast.

❖ Trial in advance: Practice makes perfect, and this is especially true for podcasting. Do a few test recordings before you start recording your guests. This will help you get familiar with your microphone, recording software, and recording environment. Be sure to listen back to your test recordings and adjust your setup if needed.

❖ Maintain a good distance from the microphone: Too close

and you will cause mic distortion, too far and you'll get a hollow sound.

Avoiding common mistakes:

There are some common mistakes that podcasters make when recording. These can be simple things that are easy to fix, but if you don't catch them in advance, they can spoil your entire recording. Here are a few of the most common mistakes to watch out for:

- ❖ Hitting the microphone or headset with your fingers or other objects. This can cause noise or distortion that ruins your audio quality.

- ❖ Speaking into the top or the sides of your microphone. Speak directly in front of the mic to improve sound quality.

- ❖ Not using headphones while recording. Feedback can creep through, and without monitor levels, you can have overs, which is when audio levels are too high and causes distorted sound.

Backing up your recordings:

It's essential to back up your recordings regularly. You don't want to lose all of your hard work due to a technical glitch or computer malfunction. Make sure you have a backup system in place to ensure that all of your episodes and important files are stored in a secure location. You can use a cloud storage service or an external hard drive as backup storage options. Whichever you choose, make sure to back up all your files every time you record a new episode.

Preparing for remote interviews:

If you plan to have remote interviews for your podcast, make sure you have used the correct tools and software to ensure good sound quality. You may need to download a video communication app and make sure you have good internet connectivity. You and your guests should wear headphones with built-in microphones to avoid feedback and echoes. By taking care of the technical details beforehand, you'll have a smooth interview experience.

Conducting interviews:

Conducting an interview can be challenging. The best interviews are the ones that feel like a natural conversation. Show genuine interest and enthusiasm for your guests and their work. Listen attentively and ask relevant follow-up questions. Avoid monosyllabic responses, as they can shut down a conversation. An interview is a two-way conversation so don't dominate the conversation. Depending on the guest's pace, aim to record for between 30-60 minutes.

Microphone techniques:

Microphone techniques might sound fancy or challenging, but they're actually quite simple. Generally, the rule is to speak into the mic while keeping your distance. Don't forget to breathe and avoid sharp intakes of breath that can cause awkward sounds to appear. Depending on your style of the podcast, you may want to experiment with different techniques to find what works best for you. The best thing to do is to experiment and practice different techniques to find what works best for you.

Monitor levels and avoiding clipping:

When recording, it's important to monitor your audio levels to avoid clipping. Clipping happens when the sound of the audio suddenly and sharply jumps off the scale during the recording. This can cause distorted audio levels and permanently damage the equipment. You need to ensure that your levels stay consistent and avoid getting too high or too low. By regularly checking your levels and using meters to monitor the sound, you can avoid clipping, and the overall quality of your sound will be much better.

Conclusion:

Recording is the core of your podcast episode, and by adopting best practices, avoiding common mistakes, and backing up your recordings, you will ensure a better sound quality for your podcast. You can have a great conversation, but if the sound quality is awful, you'll lose listeners instantly. By taking the time to invest and improve your recording techniques, you'll produce higher quality content, and that's what matters most when it comes to podcasting.

CHAPTER 6: EDITING

Now that you've recorded all your content, it's time to edit your podcast and create a polished final product. Editing is an important aspect of podcasting, as it can help improve the flow of the show and make it more engaging for listeners. In this chapter, we will discuss some basic editing techniques, common editing mistakes, and how to avoid them.

Basic Editing Techniques

Before you begin editing, you should have a basic understanding of how to use editing software. There are many editing software options available, ranging from free options like Audacity to more professional tools like Adobe Audition or Pro Tools.

Once you have your software installed and your files imported, you can begin editing. A good first step is to listen to your recording in its entirety and take notes on areas that need to be improved or removed. This can include long pauses, stuttering, or mistakes.

Trimming, Cutting and Pasting Clips

To trim an audio clip, select the section of audio you want to remove and press the delete key. This is useful for removing long pauses or mistakes.

To cut a section of audio, select the section you want to remove and then press the cut or copy command in your editing software. You can then paste the section elsewhere in your recording or delete it entirely.

Adding Music and Sound Effects

Adding music and sound effects can enhance the overall quality of your podcast. You can use royalty-free music and sound effects from websites like SoundCloud or Freesound. When adding music or sound effects, make sure they are appropriate for the context of your podcast and don't overwhelm your content.

Enhancing Audio Quality

You can enhance the audio quality of your podcast with filters. These filters can help remove unwanted noise, boost quiet sections or reduce background hum. Experiment with different filters to find what works best for your recording.

Removing Unwanted Noise

Unwanted noise can be distracting for your listeners and can ruin the quality of your podcast. To remove unwanted noise, use a noise reduction filter in your editing software. This will allow you to select the portion of audio you want to filter and remove unwanted background noise.

Adding Intros and Outros

Intros and outros can help create consistency across your episodes and give your podcast a professional feel. You can record your intros and outros separately and then add them to your recordings in your editing software. Make sure your intros and outros are short and to the point and capture the essence of your podcast.

Common Editing Mistakes and How to Avoid Them

Editing can be time-consuming, and mistakes can happen. Here are some common editing mistakes and how to avoid them:

- ❖ Removing too much content: While editing, be careful not to remove too much content, as this can disrupt the flow of your podcast and remove important information.

- ❖ Over-editing: Over-editing can make your podcast sound unnatural, so try to keep it as natural as possible.

- ❖ Failing to listen to the entire recording: Make sure you listen to the entire recording before editing, as this can help you identify areas that need to be improved.

- ❖ Rushing the editing process: Editing takes time, so don't rush the process. Take breaks and come back to your editing with fresh ears.

Conclusion

Editing is an essential part of podcasting, as it can help refine your content and create a polished final product. By using basic editing techniques like trimming, cutting, and pasting clips, adding music and sound effects, enhancing audio quality, and adding intros and outros, you can improve the flow and quality of your podcast. Be sure to avoid common editing mistakes like over-editing, removing too much content, rushing the editing process, and failing to listen to the entire recording. With these tips, you can create a high-quality podcast that engages your audience and keeps them coming back for more.

CHAPTER 7: PUBLISHING & DISTRIBUTION

Starting a podcast can be a daunting task, but once you've recorded and edited your first few episodes, it's time to focus on publishing and distribution. In today's digital age, there's no shortage of platforms to host and share your podcast, but it's important to choose the right one for your needs.

Choosing a Podcast Hosting Service

A podcast hosting service is a dedicated platform where your episodes will reside. It functions as a storage space and distribution network for your podcast. When a listener clicks on your podcast link, the hosting service delivers the audio file to them. Most hosting services charge a monthly or yearly fee, but there are also some free options available.

When choosing a hosting service, consider the following factors:

❖ Price: Hosting fees can range from a few dollars per month to hundreds of dollars per year based on the size of your podcast.

❖ Storage Limitations: Check the hosting service's storage limits and make sure they can accommodate your growing podcast library.

❖ Bandwidth: Make sure the hosting service can handle the number of downloads you expect to receive. If your podcast becomes popular, you'll need a hosting service that can accommodate an influx of traffic.

❖ Analytics: Look for a hosting service that provides detailed analytics on your podcast's performance, such as the number of downloads, demographic breakdowns, and listener behaviour.

❖ Customer Support: Consider a hosting service with strong customer support, such as email, phone, or live chat, to assist you with any technical issues.

Some of the most popular podcast hosting services include Libsyn, Buzzsprout, and Podbean. Each has its own pricing structure, features, and benefits, so do some research before making a decision.

Uploading Your Podcast to the Hosting Service

Once you've chosen a hosting service, it's time to upload your podcast. Most hosting services have a simple drag-and-drop interface for uploading your episodes, but some may require you to use FTP or an API.

When uploading your episodes, make sure they meet the hosting service's requirements for file type, length, and size. Some services may limit the number of episodes you can upload at once, so ensure you plan accordingly.

Setting Up RSS Feeds

Once you've uploaded your podcast episodes to your chosen hosting service, you'll need to set up an RSS (Really Simple Syndication) feed. An RSS feed is a web feed that allows users and systems to access and receive updates on your podcast automatically.

Your hosting service will typically provide you with an RSS feed link that you can submit to podcast directories like iTunes and Spotify. It's important to ensure your RSS feed is correctly formatted and includes key information about your podcast, such as your logo, title, description, and category.

Submitting Your Podcast to Directories

Submitting your podcast to directories is the best way to increase its visibility and attract new listeners. Most directories require an RSS feed to list your podcast, so make sure your feed is set up correctly before submitting your podcast.

iTunes is the largest directory for podcasts, accounting for over 70% of all downloads. To submit your podcast to iTunes, you'll need an Apple ID, a podcast artwork image, and your RSS feed link. Once you've submitted your podcast, it can take up to 10 days to be reviewed and approved.

Other directories such as Spotify, Stitcher, and Google Play have different submission requirements, so check their specifications and guidelines before submitting your podcast.

Creating Show Notes

Show notes are an essential component of your podcast, providing listeners with an overview of the episode's content and links to related resources. They also improve your podcast's visibility on search engines by including relevant keywords.

When creating show notes, consider the following:

➢ Title: Make sure the title accurately reflects the content of the episode and includes relevant keywords.

➢ Summary: Summarise the episode's main points and

include timestamps for key sections.

➢ Links: Include links to any resources or websites mentioned in the episode.

➢ Call-to-Action: Encourage listeners to review your podcast, subscribe, or leave feedback.

Promoting Your Podcast on Social Media

Social media is a powerful tool for promoting your podcast and connecting with your audience. By sharing your episodes on Facebook, Twitter, Instagram, LinkedIn, and other platforms, you can reach a broader audience and increase your followers.

Some tips for promoting your podcast on social media include:

➢ Creating eye-catching graphics to highlight your episode's content.

➢ Using relevant hashtags to reach new audiences.

➢ Sharing quotes or soundbites from the episode.

➢ Running social media contests or giveaways to engage followers.

➢ Collaborating with other podcasters or influencers.

➢ Encouraging listeners to share your podcast with their friends and followers.

Leveraging Your Existing Audience

Your existing audience is an invaluable asset for promoting and growing your podcast. Encourage your listeners to review and rate your podcast, share it with their friends and family, and provide feedback on each episode.

Some ways to leverage your existing audience include:

➤ Encouraging listeners to subscribe to your podcast.

➤ Asking listeners to review your podcast on platforms like iTunes.

➤ Providing a call-to-action at the end of each episode, asking listeners to share your podcast with their network.

➤ Sharing user-generated content from your listeners on social media.

➤ Offering exclusive content or bonuses to your existing audience.

Developing a Distribution Strategy

Creating a distribution strategy means approaching the promotion and distribution of your podcast as you would a marketing campaign. By developing a distribution strategy, you can leverage multiple channels to reach new audiences, including email marketing, social media, paid advertising, influencers, and partnerships.

When developing your distribution strategy, consider the following:

➤ Your target audience: Who are you trying to reach with your podcast, and where do they consume content?

➤ Your budget: How much can you allocate to paid advertising or other promotional activities?

➤ Your channels: Which marketing channels (email, social media, partnerships, etc.) are most effective for reaching your audience?

➤ Your messaging: What key messages do you want to convey

to your audience, and how can you effectively communicate them?

➢   Your timeline: What is your timeline for promoting your podcast, and how will you measure success?

By developing a distribution strategy, you can ensure that your podcast reaches the right audience and maximises its potential for growth and success.

CHAPTER 8: MONETISATION STRATEGIES

Congratulations! You've successfully launched your podcast, grown your audience, and built a community around your content. Now it's time to monetize your podcast and turn your passion into a source of income. In this chapter, we'll explore different monetization strategies you can use to generate revenue and build a sustainable business around your podcast.

Sponsorships and Advertising

One of the most common ways to monetize a podcast is through sponsorships and advertising. Advertisers are always looking for new audiences to reach, and podcasts provide a highly engaged and loyal listener base. When you partner with a sponsor, they'll typically give you a script or talking points to read during your show, and you'll get paid per ad spot or per episode. You can also choose to sell ad space on your own through platforms like Advertisecast or Podbean.

Crowdfunding

If you're just starting out, crowdfunding can be a great way to fund your podcast and build a community around your content. Platforms like Patreon, Kickstarter, or IndieGoGo allow your listeners to support your podcast with small monthly donations or one-time contributions. In exchange, you can offer exclusive content or perks like early access to episodes, merchandise, or shout-outs on your show.

Merchandising

Selling merchandise can be a lucrative revenue stream for podcasters with a dedicated fan base. You can create branded merchandise like t-shirts, mugs, stickers, or even your own line of products. Platforms like Teespring, Redbubble, or Printful let you design and sell your merchandise without needing a large upfront investment or inventory.

Donations

If your listeners love your content and want to support your podcast, you can also accept donations through PayPal or Patreon. Some podcasters even set up a donation page on their website or create a "Buy Me a Coffee" account, where listeners can contribute a few dollars to show their appreciation. Make sure to be transparent about how the donations will be used and express gratitude to your supporters.

Affiliate Marketing

Affiliate marketing is a popular way to monetize podcasts, especially if you have a niche audience. You can partner with companies that offer products or services related to your podcast's topic and promote them to your listeners. When someone clicks on your affiliate link and makes a purchase, you'll earn a commission. Platforms like Amazon Associates, ShareASale, or Commission Junction offer thousands of affiliate programs to join.

Selling Premium Content

If you have valuable content that your listeners are willing to pay for, you can create a premium subscription or membership program. This could include bonus episodes, exclusive interviews, behind-the-scenes content, or access to a private community or forum. Platforms like Patreon, Supercast, or Glow.fm offer tools to create and manage premium content subscriptions.

Licensing Content

If you've built a sizeable library of content, you can also license it to third-party platforms, such as audiobook publishers, audio streaming services, or syndication networks. This can be an excellent way to generate passive income and increase your exposure to new audiences.

Brand Partnerships

Finally, you can also partner with other brands or creators in your industry to collaborate on projects or sponsorships. This could include joint events, co-branded content, or cross-promotions. Make sure to choose brand partners that align with your values and have similar audiences to yours.

Overall, there are many ways to monetize a podcast, and the best strategy will depend on your podcast's topic, audience, and goals. Don't be afraid to experiment with different approaches and track your results to find what works best for you. As your podcast grows, you may discover new revenue opportunities and build a sustainable business around your passion.

CHAPTER 9: BUILDING YOUR PODCAST TEAM

Starting your podcast journey may seem like a one-man show, but it's not. Building a team is essential to scaling and growing your podcast to achieve your long-term goals. A team brings different skill sets, ideas, and perspectives to the table, resulting in high-quality podcasts. In this chapter, we'll discuss how to find, hire, and manage your team members, including co-hosts, guests, and freelancers.

Identifying roles and responsibilities

The first step to building your dream team is identifying the roles and responsibilities. You can't build a team without knowing what you need. The roles you assign to your team will vary depending on the nature of your podcast and your goals. Here are some typical team roles:

- ❖ Host: The host is the face and voice of your podcast. They guide the conversation and keep things flowing smoothly.

- ❖ Co-host: A co-host brings another perspective to the podcast and can help you share the workload.

- ❖ Producer: The producer is responsible for recording, editing, and publishing the podcast.

- ❖ Audio Engineer: An audio engineer works with the sound to ensure that the audio quality is top-notch.

❖ Social Media Manager: The social media manager is responsible for promoting the podcast on different social media platforms.

❖ Researcher: A researcher gathers information, prepares show notes, script outline, and helps with content development.

❖ Guest Booker: A guest booker is responsible for finding and scheduling guests for interviews.

❖ Marketing Manager: A marketing manager works to promote and grow your podcast through different marketing strategies.

Finding and hiring talent

Finding the right talent for your podcast is crucial to your success. Here are some tips on finding and hiring the right people for your team:

➤ Use job boards, freelance websites, and social media platforms like LinkedIn to find potential candidates.

➤ Look for candidates with relevant skills and experiences.

➤ Try to evaluate their past work and references.

➤ When hiring, look for people who are passionate about your podcast and your niche.

➤ Be open to working with freelancers or outsourcing some tasks to external professionals.

Building relationships with guests

Guests are essential to your podcast as they provide valuable insights, experiences, and stories. Building a good relationship with your guests is crucial to getting them to come back and being advocates of your podcast.

➢ Make your guests feel welcome and comfortable before the interview.

➢ Provide clear instructions and guidelines before the interview.

➢ Build a rapport beforehand and connect with your guests through social media.

➢ Follow up with your guests after the interview to thank them and to gather feedback on their experience.

Recruiting co-hosts

Having a co-host can bring new energy, ideas, and insights to your podcast. When recruiting a co-host, here are some things to keep in mind:

❖ Look for someone who shares your passion and interest in your niche and topic.

❖ Evaluate the chemistry between you and your co-host before committing to working together.

❖ Clearly identify the responsibilities and expectations for both co-hosts.

❖ Be open to feedback and be willing to adapt to the needs of your co-host.

Delegating tasks

When building your team, you need to be careful about delegating tasks. Delegating tasks can free up time and enable you to focus on creating high-quality content. However, delegating tasks can also be problematic if not done correctly.

❖ Divide the tasks based on each team member's strengths and skills.

❖   Clearly communicate the deadlines, expectations, and feedback mechanisms.

❖   Regularly check in with the team to ensure that the work is on-track.

❖   Avoid micromanaging and allow people to do their jobs.

Creating a community around your podcast

Creating a community around your podcast can help build engagement and loyalty from listeners. A community can also help you get feedback and ideas for improving your podcast. Here are some ways to create a community around your podcast:

❖   Encourage listeners to engage with you on social media by asking for their feedback, comments, and questions.

❖   Create a Facebook group to allow listeners to connect with each other and provide feedback.

❖   Host live events or Q and A sessions to connect with your listeners.

❖   Establish a newsletter to keep your listeners informed about updates, new episodes, and behind-the-scenes content.

Managing conflict

When building a team, conflicts may arise, and it's vital to manage them appropriately. Here are a few tips on managing conflict:

❖   Listen to both sides and understand the issue before reacting.

❖   Communicate clearly to ensure that everyone is on the same page.

❖   Avoid blame and instead focus on finding a solution.

❖ Be willing to compromise and find common ground.

Scaling the team for growth

As your podcast grows, so will your team. Scaling your team is essential to achieve your broader goals for your podcast. Here are some tips on scaling your team for growth:

❖ Identify new roles that you need to add to your team to achieve your goals.

❖ Identify the skills and experiences required for these new roles.

❖ Set up a hiring process that is scalable and repeatable.

❖ Continuously evaluate and optimize your team to ensure they are performing optimally.

In conclusion, building a team is critical to your podcast's long-term success. Building a team takes time, effort, and patience. However, the benefits of having a team can be significant and include increased productivity, better quality podcasts, and a sense of community. With the tips above, you are on your way to building your dream team.

CHAPTER 10: MEASURING SUCCESS

You've successfully launched your podcast and now have a loyal audience. You may wonder how you can measure the success of your show, and whether it's worth the time and effort you put in. With podcasting becoming a crowded space, having a way to gauge your performance and adapt to user feedback is essential.

Setting KPIs for Your Podcast

KPIs or Key Performance Indicators helps to measure the success of your podcast. They help identify how well your podcast is performing in terms of audience retention, brand recognition, listener base, and other metrics. Identifying the key metrics and having measurable KPIs will guide you in pivoting your strategy, improving the content quality, and aligning efforts towards the desired goals.

Some of the common KPIs include:

➢   Number of downloads: It's the most basic metric that defines the popularity of any podcast. The number of downloads, in a way, is indicative of the reach of your podcast.

➢ Subscribers: This metric reveals the number of people who have signed up to receive regular updates on your shows. It is an essential metric to consider while negotiating for sponsorship deals.

> Listener retention rate: This metric shows what percentage of your audience listens to the whole show and when they usually drop off. It can give you an idea of the length of your show, segments, and average attention span of your listeners.

> Audience engagement: Engagement can be in the form of shares on social media, comments, likes, and ratings. It is an important metric to consider while planning promotions and collaborations with other brands.

> Brand recognition: This metric helps you measure how well your podcast is known within your niche. It is possible to gauge brand recognition by monitoring the number of mentions your brand gets on social media and press.

Measuring Engagement

Engagement is one of the most important metrics that help in building a loyal audience. When your listeners are engaged, they are more likely to leave reviews, suggest stories, and share information related to your podcast. There are several ways to measure engagement for your podcast:

❖ Social media: Social media can be a great way to interact with listeners, understand feedback, and measure engagement. You can monitor your social media mentions, likes, shares, and use social media analytics tools to understand how your content is received on these platforms.

❖ Surveys and feedback sessions: You can reach out to your listeners via surveys and feedback sessions to know what works and what doesn't work for your show. You can use these sessions to gauge how your listeners feel about your content.

❖ Email campaigns: Emails may be considered an old-school tactic, but they are still effective in generating engagement. You can use email campaigns to keep your listeners informed about new episodes, special events, promotions, and other interesting stories.

Understanding Analytics

Analytics can seem overwhelming at first, but they are critical in refining your podcast strategy. Analytics can help you make data-backed decisions and continually improve your show. Some of the most common analytics tools to consider are:

❖ buzzsprout: It's a robust hosting platform that lets you monitor and track insights about your podcast's performance. It allows you to track the traffic sources, number of listens, and insights on audience engagement in real-time.

❖ Google Analytics: Google Analytics allows you to measure traffic and user behavior on your website. By diving into this data, you can gain insights into the demographics of your listeners, including where they access your podcast.

❖ Mixpanel: Mixpanel lets you analyze your listener's behavior using parameters like clicks, scrolls, and other user events. By analyzing this data, you can optimize your content, user experience, and engagement levels.

Developing a Metrics Dashboard

A metrics dashboard is a tool that helps you track your podcast metrics in a single place. When tracking data, less is often more. You don't want to measure too much and end up with overwhelming data. The dashboard should have a few key metrics that are aligned with your podcast's goals. You can consider using a metrics dashboard to measure the following:

❖ Total downloads and subscribers

❖ Monthly active listeners

❖ Listener retention rates

❖ User behavior on your website or social media

❖ Number of revenue streams and revenue generated

❖ Feedback collected from your listeners.

Adapting to Feedback

Feedback is essential in improving your podcast. It helps you know what's working and what's not working with your listeners. Many podcasters shy away from feedback since it's not always what they want to hear. But feedback should be taken as an opportunity to improve and grow. Here's how to adapt to feedback:

➢ Listen actively: When receiving feedback, listen actively to what the listener is saying. Try to understand the context and underlying concerns that they are conveying.

➢ Acknowledge feedback: It's important to acknowledge the feedback received, whether in the form of an email, comment, or review. It encourages the listener to keep the conversation going and shows that you value their opinions.

➢ Implement changes based on feedback: Implementing changes based on feedback shows that you are taking it seriously. It also helps in building a better connection with your audience. Sometimes the changes don't necessarily align with your strategy, so evaluate it before incorporating it.

➢ Tell your listeners: Once you've implemented the changes that your listeners have suggested, tell them. Creating a post updating listeners about the changes shows that you value their opinions and motivates them to keep engaging with your content.

Conclusion

Measuring success in podcasting requires a strategy, time, and effort, and it is not an overnight progress. It requires tracking relevant data, setting KPIs, and adapting to feedback. Continuously tracking metrics, analyzing data, and adapting to feedback is key to improving the quality of your content and fostering engagement with your audience. By carefully tracking and analyzing data, you can watch your podcast grow, find new opportunities, and discover new ways to monetize your content.

CHAPTER 11: LEGAL CONSIDERATIONS

Congratulations! You have created a captivating podcast which has now gained considerable traction among listeners. And the revenue stream has started to build up. That's great news, right? But have you considered the legal implications of running a show? In this chapter, we will discuss several legal considerations that every podcaster should understand.

Copyright and fair use

As a podcaster, you must ensure that you have permission to use copyrighted material, such as music and sound effects, in your show. You can either purchase a license to use them, use royalty-free options or use material in the public domain. In some cases, you might be able to use clips under "fair use" exceptions, but you should consult with a lawyer to ensure that you are not infringing on anyone's rights.

Music licensing

Music licensing for podcasts can be complicated, especially if you want to use popular songs from major artists. You will need to secure the proper licenses from the appropriate music rights organizations. You should also be aware that licensing requirements can differ depending on the platform, so you need to do your research.

Trademarks and branding

When creating your podcast brand, it is important to ensure that you are not infringing on any trademarks. You should always conduct a trademark search before using any names, logos, or slogans to verify that you are not infringing on any existing intellectual property rights. You should also apply to register your trademark with the relevant trademark authority to prevent others from misusing it.

Privacy and data protection

As a podcaster, you are likely to collect personal data from your listeners, such as their email addresses and names. You must ensure that you are complying with the relevant data protection laws. You should also have a clear privacy policy detailing how you collect, use, and protect the personal data of your listeners.

Advertising disclosure rules

If your podcast includes advertising or sponsorship, you must disclose that fact to your listeners. Failure to do so can result in the loss of credibility and trust among your audience. The Federal Trade Commission (FTC) in the United States requires you to disclose any sponsorships or ads that you receive.

Defamation

As a podcaster, you should not make defamatory comments about anyone in your podcast. Defamation can refer to making false statements that could cause damage to someone's reputation, character, or creditworthiness. If you do make such statements, you can be sued for defamation.

Employment and contractor agreements

If you hire people to help you produce your podcast, you should have written contracts in place outlining the terms of the agreement between you and the people you hire. The contract should clearly establish the scope of work, responsibilities, payment terms, and confidentiality obligations.

Insurance requirements

When running a podcast, there are several insurance policies that you would need to consider such as General Liability insurance if you are recording at an event and need protection against lawsuits resulting from injuries, Property Insurance to get protection for your computer, microphone, and any equipment used to record and produce your podcast interview, and Cyber Liability insurance if you host guest interviews through platforms like Skype, Google Hangouts, or Zoom. You should consult with a commercial insurance broker who specializes in the media & entertainment industry.

In conclusion, failure to pay attention to legal considerations can result in lawsuits and significant financial risk. Understanding the legal landscape will ensure that you establish a legally compliant and professional podcast. Consult with a lawyer, in case of any ambiguity.

CHAPTER 12: GROWING YOUR AUDIENCE

Once you have created and uploaded your podcast, it's time to focus on growing your audience. While producing great content is essential, your audience won't magically appear out of nowhere. In this chapter, we will discuss various strategies to increase your listenership and grow your audience.

Creating Compelling Content

The most important aspect of growing your podcast audience is creating high-quality content that your listeners will love. Take the time to plan your episodes and ensure that your content is engaging, informative, and entertaining. Be authentic and true to your style and brand and provide value to your listeners.

One effective way to improve your content is by researching your audience. Conduct surveys and engage your audience in conversation on social media platforms. You can also monitor your analytics to understand which episodes or topics resonated most with your listeners.

Audience Engagement

Engaging with your listeners can help your podcast grow. One effective way to do this is by asking for feedback, such as through surveys or on social media platforms. Responding to listener comments and messages also helps to build a relationship with your audience. If you can, add listener questions to your podcast, which will make them feel heard and involved.

User-Generated Content

Engage your audience to create user-generated content surrounding your podcast. This can include reviews, feedback, artwork or even listener mail episodes. When your listeners feel that they are a part of your community, they are more likely to promote and share your content with their network. So, make sure that you use these materials or spotlight them on your public platforms.

Interviewing Thought Leaders

Inviting a thought leader in your field as a guest on your podcast can have many advantages. Not only do they bring credibility to your podcast, but they can also help to promote your podcast to their audience with a wider reach. Networking with thought leaders in your niche and inviting them to be a guest on your podcast can attract new listeners who are interested in your topic.

Cross-Promotion

Cross-promotion is a strategy where two or more podcasts work together to promote each other's shows. For example, a running podcast can team up with a nutrition podcast to promote each other's episodes. It's a win-win situation as both podcasts can benefit from each other's audience reach.

Referral Marketing

Another effective way to grow your podcast audience is through referral marketing. Encourage your listeners to share episodes with their friends and family, either by word-of-mouth or on social media. Offering incentives such as a giveaway for every five referrals can motivate your audience to promote your podcast and attract new listeners.

Interacting with Listeners

Beyond asking for feedback, engaging with listeners can take many forms. You can create Facebook groups or channels dedicated to discussing your topics, which provides a space for your audience to discuss with each other. You can also hold Q&A sessions, where your listeners can ask you questions. Hosting live events can also allow you to meet your listeners and network with them. Organizing meetups with your listeners is not only an excellent way to connect with them but also a way to build your community.

Leveraging Social Media Platforms

Social media is an excellent platform to promote your podcast, engage with listeners, network with other podcasters, and grow your audience. Find and join relevant groups and follow the hashtags in your niche relevant to your podcast. Create compelling visuals and shareable content that can generate buzz around your episodes. Use the analytics of these platforms to optimise your content, posting time, audience demographics, and interests.

Conclusion

Growing your podcast audience takes time, effort, and patience. A solid content strategy, audience engagement, user-generated content, interviewing thought leaders, cross-promotion, referral marketing, interacting with your listeners and leveraging social media can all make a difference in growing your listenership. Keep in mind that creating value for your listeners should always be at the forefront of your podcast strategy. When you make an effort to create high-quality content that resonates with your target audience, your podcast will begin to grow organically.

CHAPTER 13: STAYING RELEVANT

In the fast-moving world of podcasting, staying relevant is a challenge that every podcaster faces. With new trends, changing audience needs, and evolving technologies, it's important to keep your show fresh and engaging. In this chapter, we'll explore some strategies for staying relevant and maintaining the high quality of your podcast.

Keeping up with Industry Trends

To stay relevant, it's important to keep up with industry trends and shifts in listener behavior. One way to do this is by attending industry events and conferences, where you can connect with other podcasters and industry experts. You can also keep an eye on industry publications, such as Podcast Business Journal and PodNews, to stay up-to-date with the latest news, trends, and insights.

Aside from industry events and publications, you can also participate in online communities and forums to stay informed about the latest tools and tactics that other podcasters are using. Facebook Groups, Reddit, and LinkedIn Groups are all great places to stay connected with other podcasters and industry experts. By staying engaged in the community, you'll be able to share best practices, learn from others, and get inspired.

Evolving Your Show Format

To keep your show exciting and fresh, it's important to experiment with new ideas and try out different formats. This could mean changing up your show's length, introducing new segments, or even pivoting your show to a new topic. For example, you could consider adding video content to your podcast to give your listeners a new way to engage with your show.

Another way to evolve your show format is to incorporate listener feedback and ideas. Encourage your listeners to share their thoughts and ideas with you and incorporate their feedback into future episodes. You could also consider creating listener polls or surveys to get a better understanding of what your listeners enjoy and what they want to hear more of.

Adapting to Changing Audience Needs

As your listenership grows and changes, it's important to adapt to their changing needs. This may involve creating new types of content, such as bonus episodes or spin-off series. Look for opportunities to engage with your audience in new ways and keep them coming back for more.

To stay in touch with your audience's changing needs, consider expanding your social media presence, or offering exclusive content through a Patreon or membership program. This will enable you to build a deeper relationship with your listeners, who will be more likely to stick around and engage with your show over time.

Incorporating Audience Feedback

One of the most valuable resources for staying relevant is audience feedback. Take the time to engage with your listeners and respond to their comments and feedback – even if it's negative or critical. By incorporating audience feedback into your show, you'll be able to improve your content and keep your listeners engaged.

To collect feedback, consider creating a feedback form on your website or encouraging listeners to email you directly. You could also engage with listeners on social media or during live events, or even try out a call-in segment on your show. Once you've collected feedback, take the time to analyze it and prioritize the changes that will have the most impact on your show.

Experimenting with New Ideas

In addition to evolving your show format, it's important to experiment with new ideas and approaches. This could mean trying out new topics, inviting new guest speakers, or even incorporating new technologies, such as virtual reality or live-streaming.

To generate new ideas, consider brainstorming sessions with your team, attending creative workshops or taking online courses. You could also ask for input from your listeners or collaborate with other podcasters to explore new topics and formats.

Collaborating with Other Podcasters

Another way to stay relevant is to collaborate with other podcasters. Collaborations can provide a fresh perspective on topics, expand your listenership and grow your network. When collaborating, try to find podcasters whose content aligns with your audience and your niche.

To collaborate effectively, make sure to clearly define your goals and expectations and establish a clear workflow. You could consider co-hosting an episode, cross-promoting each other's podcasts, or even guesting on each other's shows.

Being Open to Constructive Criticism

One of the most important traits for staying relevant is to be open to feedback and constructive criticism. By being open to new ideas and feedback, you'll be able to adapt and improve your podcast to meet your audience's needs and stay ahead of the curve.

To build your resilience to criticism, try to adopt a growth mindset and view feedback as an opportunity for improvement. It's also important to remember that not all feedback will be constructive or useful, and it's okay to filter out comments that aren't helpful or actionable.

Constantly Learning and Improving

Finally, to stay ahead of the curve, it's important to adopt a mindset of continuous learning and improvement. This could mean taking online courses, attending conferences or workshops, or even just reading industry publications and subscribing to your competitors' podcasts.

To make the most of your learning efforts, try to invest time in developing specific skill sets, such as audio editing, video editing, or content strategy. Identify areas that are relevant to your niche and your audience and focus on developing your expertise in these areas.

In conclusion, staying relevant in the ever-evolving world of podcasting requires ongoing adaptation, experimentation, and improvement. By staying engaged with your audience, keeping up with industry trends and exploring new ideas, you'll be able to stay ahead of the curve and keep your podcast fresh and exciting for years to come.

CHAPTER 14: DEVELOPING A MARKETING PLAN

Congratulations, you have created your podcast! Now, how do you get people to listen to it? The answer is simple: you need a marketing plan. In this chapter, we will discuss the various strategies that you can employ to market your podcast successfully. From content and email marketing to influencer collaborations and even live event promotion, there are numerous ways to get your podcast in front of your target audience.

Identify Your Target Audience

Your target audience is the group of people who will most appreciate your podcast. Before you create any marketing plan, you need to identify who these individuals are. Once you have done so, you can tailor your message and approach to suit their tastes and preferences.

Start by creating a clear listener persona. This is a detailed profile of your ideal listener that includes demographic information such as age, gender, income, interests, and habits. You can use this persona to shape your marketing message and refine your approach.

Create A Content Strategy

Your content is the backbone of your podcast, and it's critical to create a consistent schedule of interesting and relevant content that will keep your listeners engaged. When marketing your podcast, you can use your existing content to attract new listeners and to build your brand.

Start by creating a content calendar that outlines the topics you'll cover in each episode. You can use this calendar to plan your marketing messages and craft social media posts that promote your upcoming episodes. Additionally, consider leveraging guest interviews and collaborations to enhance your content and boost your marketing reach.

Create A Mailing List

A mailing list is a valuable marketing tool for podcasters. It allows you to communicate directly with your listeners and to keep them informed about upcoming episodes and promotions. A mailing list is easy to build - simply include a signup form on your website or promote it on social media.

When creating your mailing list, focus on creating targeted and valuable content. Avoid sending out promotional messages only and instead, offer your subscribers useful tips, insights, or exclusive content through email.

Promote On Social Media

Social media is one of the most effective ways to market your podcast to new listeners. You can use your social media profiles to promote your episodes, engage with your listeners, and even collaborate with influencers.

Start by identifying the most popular social networks for your target audience. Depending on your content, this may include Facebook, Twitter, Instagram, or LinkedIn. Share snippets from your episodes, post behind-the-scenes content, and engage with your followers to build your community. Additionally, consider collaborations with influencers and other podcasters to expand your reach.

Start A Blog

A podcast blog offers you an opportunity to expand your audience, drive traffic to your website, and establish yourself as an authority in your niche. Here are a few tips to help you get started:

- ➤ Create fresh and engaging content that is related to your podcast topics.

- ➤ Use your blog to boost your SEO (Search engine optimization).

- ➤ Cross-promote your blog posts and podcast on social media.

Keep in mind, however, that blogging can be time-consuming. Consider hiring a freelance writer or editor to help you create high-quality content.

Run Ads

Ads can be another effective way to promote your podcast. Here are a few things to consider when running your ads:

- ➤ Choose a platform that has a large audience of your target listener.

- ➤ Design eye-catching creatives that align with your brand and message.

- ➤ Identify your bidding strategy, ensuring that your ads only reach those who are likely to listen to your podcast.

Hosting Live Events

Hosting live events can be a powerful way to connect with your listeners in-person and to build brand recognition. Here are a few things to consider when planning your live event:

> Choose a venue and event type that aligns with your brand message and niche.

> Make sure that your event is accessible to your target listener demographic.

> Promote your event through your existing channels, including your podcast, social media, blog, and email list.

Additionally, consider offering merchandise or access via premium access, to attract your listeners and to increase your revenue stream.

Leveraging Influencer Marketing

Influencer marketing has become increasingly popular in recent years. This marketing strategy involves partnering with influencers in your niche to promote your podcast to their followers.

When searching for influencers, focus on those who are likely to align with your message and brand. For example, if you run a business podcast, look for influencers who are established in the business community. Reach out to them with a compelling message and offer to collaborate on a promotion. On completion of the promotion, make sure to monitor your analytics and measure any changes in your listenership.

Conclusion

Developing a marketing plan for your podcast does not have to be complicated. By focusing on your target audience, content strategy, social media, and collaborations, you can create a plan that resonates with your listeners and promotes growth.

Marketing your podcast can take time, effort, and possibly some creativity. Remember to experiment with different approaches and strategies, and don't be afraid to adapt your approach as needed. With the right marketing and promotions, you can grow your podcast audience, increase your listeners, and enhance your brand's exposure.

CHAPTER 15: CREATING ENGAGING CONTENT

Congratulations! You have set up your podcast, chosen a unique selling proposition, and defined your brand. Now, the focus is on creating engaging content.

As a podcast host, you should aim to keep your audience entertained while providing valuable information. The key is to be engaging, relatable, and authentic. Here are some tips to help you create great content:

Storytelling Techniques

Humans have been telling stories for centuries, and it remains a potent way to engage your audience. When you narrate stories, be it personal anecdotes or case studies, paint a picture with your words. Engage your audience's imagination and make them feel like they are part of the story. That way, they can relate to what you are saying and feel invested in your podcast.

Compelling Titles

The first element of any episode that your listeners will see is the titles of your episodes. Therefore, creating an attention-grabbing title is crucial. Your title should be catchy, informative, and easy to remember. You can also use keywords in your title to optimize for search engines. Keep in mind the 80-20 rule - 80% of episode titles should be informative, and 20% should be entertaining.

Using Guest Interviews Effectively

Having guests on your podcast can be an excellent way to expand your reach and provide unique perspectives. Interviewing guests is not about you. Still, it involves creating conditions where guests can share their expertise and be as engaging as possible. There are some essential steps to follow:

> ➤ Do your research: When preparing for a guest interview, make sure that you know enough about the guest's background, the topic, and their perspectives.

> ➤ Create a script or a structure: It's okay to have a structure or outline for the interview but be spontaneous too.

> ➤ Provide context: Start the interview with some context and make it as concise as possible.

> ➤ Prepare open-ended questions: Since you want your guests to be engaging and share their opinions, it's best to ask open-ended questions.

> ➤ Be present: While interviewing, paying attention to what the guest is saying and respond accordingly.

Effective Call-to-Actions

At the end of each episode, you should give your listeners a reason to return. Providing clear call-to-actions can help you do that and encourage listeners to share your episodes or leave a review. Common calls-to-action include:

- ❖ Asking listeners to subscribe to your podcast
- ❖ Inviting listeners to check out your website or social media channels

❖ Asking for feedback or reviews

Showcasing Your Personality

When it comes to podcasting, you are the star of your show. You should showcase your personality and provide your unique perspective on a particular topic. Personalising your podcast can help you to be more relatable to your listeners. Also, your listeners are more likely to return if they feel a personal connection.

Providing Value and Entertainment

Your podcast should be a blend of information and entertainment. You should aim to educate your listeners about something they did not know before and entertain them at the same time. Add some humour to your episodes when appropriate.

Using Humour Appropriately

Adding some humour to your episodes can help to break the monotony and keep your audience engaged. However, humour can be tricky, as it depends very much on the audience's sensitivity. Try to avoid anything too controversial or taboo. Avoid offensive jokes or making fun of people. If you decide to use humour, let it be well-timed and appropriate.

Building Anticipation for Upcoming Episodes

Make listeners look forward to the next episode by teasing what's coming up next. Use social media, teasers at the end of episodes, or include it in your show's introduction. Teasing helps to keep listeners engaged and can lead to future subscriptions.

In conclusion, creating engaging content requires a certain level of creativity, research, and the desire to make an impression. By telling compelling stories, giving your episodes catchy titles, providing valuable information, making your podcast relatable, personalising your podcast, and adding humour, when necessary, your content can stand out and attract more listeners. Don't forget to showcase your personality by being authentic and unique. Striking a balance between information and entertainment can capture your audience's attention while preparing them for forthcoming episodes.

CHAPTER 16:
NETWORKING WITH
OTHER PODCASTERS

Networking is a vital aspect of podcasting that can help in building an audience and improving the quality of content. Podcasting can often feel like a solitary endeavor, but it is essential to connect with other podcasters to share ideas, get feedback, and collaborate. In this chapter, we will delve into how to network with other podcasters in the community.

Creating relationships with other podcasters:

As a podcaster, building relationships with other podcasters is critical for growing your network and building a community. It is essential to look out for fellow podcasters who share similar interests as you and reach out to them. You can find podcasters by searching directories or social media platforms. Once you find a podcaster you would like to connect with, you can introduce yourself and invite them to listen to your podcast. You can also offer to listen to their podcast and provide feedback.

Building a network of podcasting peers:

Networking with fellow podcasters can lead to building a network of friends, collaborators, and potential guests for your show. It can be a great opportunity to brainstorm, swap ideas, and share resources. A great way to establish your network is by joining podcasting groups or forums on social media platforms like Facebook or LinkedIn. These groups give you the opportunity to interact with other podcasters, ask questions, and get feedback.

Collaborating on guest appearances:

One of the most effective ways to expand your network is through guest appearances on other podcasts. Collaborating with other podcasters allows you to reach a new audience, get feedback and build relationships with other podcasters. When guest appearing on another podcast, be sure to promote your appearance on your social media platforms and your podcast as this can lead to increased listenership.

Cross-marketing each other's shows:

Building a cross-promotional relationship with other podcasters can help promote each other's shows, guest appearances, and new content. Cross-promotion can be done by creating promos or running ads for each other's podcasts, cross-promoting social media pages, or simply by inviting guest appearances on each other's shows.

Sharing resources and best practices:

Networking can also be a great opportunity to seek help or resources from other podcasters who have more experience than you. You can share your podcast issues and ask for suggestions that will help improve the quality of your show. You can also share best practices like editing, equipment, and software.

Supporting each other's growth:

Networking with other podcasters can be incredibly valuable and rewarding. By supporting each other's growth, you can help build a sense of community within the podcasting world. As you support each other, you help improve the quality of content that is being produced in the community.

Participating in podcasting communities:

There are several opportunities to connect with other podcasters through forums, conferences, and events. Attending events or conferences can help you meet podcasters face-to-face, build relationships, and promote your show. Conferences and events are great opportunities to ask questions, get feedback and share ideas with other podcasters.

Being a guest on other shows:

As mentioned earlier, guest appearances on other podcasts can help expand your network and reach new audiences. To be a guest on another podcast, it is important to create a pitch that showcases the value you can bring to the podcast. You can approach it by highlighting the topics you will discuss, your expertise, and what the audience will learn from you.

Conclusion:

Networking with other podcasters can help improve the quality of your content, build relationships, and expand your audience. By collaborating, sharing resources, and supporting growth, podcasters can create a sense of community within the podcasting world. Networking with other podcasters means you can share ideas, learn from others, and build relationships, making podcasting a more rewarding experience.

CHAPTER 17: MANAGING YOUR TIME EFFECTIVELY

One of the biggest challenges that podcasters face is finding enough time to create and publish episodes. Many people start a podcast as a side hustle, alongside full-time jobs, family commitments, and other responsibilities. As a result, it can be difficult to stay on track and avoid burnout. In this chapter, we'll explore some tips for managing your time effectively, so that you can create great content without sacrificing your other commitments.

Creating a Podcasting Schedule

The first step in managing your time effectively is to create a schedule for your podcasting tasks. This should include time for researching, outlining, recording, editing, and publishing episodes. You may also want to include time for marketing and promotion, as well as outreach to potential guests.

When creating your podcasting schedule, be sure to take into account other commitments, such as work, family, and hobbies. It's important to be realistic about how much time you can devote to podcasting each week. Starting small and gradually building up your workload is always a good idea.

Prioritizing Tasks Effectively

Once you've created your podcasting schedule, the next step is to prioritize your tasks effectively. This means identifying the most important tasks and completing them first. For example, recording a guest interview may be more time-sensitive than editing an older episode. It's essential to focus on the tasks that will have the biggest impact on your podcast's success.

Another important aspect of prioritization is learning to say "no" to tasks that are not essential. For instance, if a potential guest doesn't align with your podcast's values or niche, it may be better to decline their invitation. This will help you stay focused on the tasks that matter most.

Keeping Track of Deadlines

It's essential to keep track of deadlines for publishing episodes, booking guests, and marketing your podcast. This can be easily done with a digital calendar or a project management tool like Trello or Asana.

Setting reminders can also be useful, either through your calendar or a smartphone app. It's important to allow enough time to complete each task without feeling overstressed or rushed.

Outsourcing Certain Tasks

If you're finding it difficult to manage your podcasting workload, outsourcing certain tasks can be a great solution. For example, you may want to hire a virtual assistant to handle administrative tasks, such as scheduling interviews or managing social media.

Editing audio files can also be a time-consuming task and outsourcing it to a professional editor can save you a lot of time and effort. It's important to weigh the costs against the benefits of outsourcing, but it can be a great way to free up more time for other tasks.

Avoiding Burnout

One of the biggest risks for podcasters is burnout. It's important to take care of yourself and avoid overloading your schedule. Make sure to take breaks, get enough sleep, and exercise regularly.

In addition, it can be helpful to schedule downtime into your podcasting schedule. This might include time to read, watch a movie, or spend time with family and friends. Give yourself permission to take a step back and recharge.

Staying Organised

Keeping your podcasting workspace organised can also be a huge time-saver. Make sure to create a system for storing and backing up your audio files, show notes, and other important documents. This can be as simple as creating folders on your computer or using a cloud-based storage system.

Creating a content calendar can also help you stay organised and plan your episodes in advance. This can reduce the stress of last-minute scrambling to find topics or guests.

Finding Balance between Podcasting and Other Commitments

Finally, it's important to find a balance between your podcasting commitments and your other responsibilities. This may require some trial and error, but finding a schedule that works for you is key to long-term success.

It's also important to communicate your podcasting commitments to your friends and family. Let them know when you're recording or editing an episode, so that they can avoid interrupting you. A little bit of planning can go a long way in helping you juggle your podcasting commitments with other priorities.

Conclusion

Managing your time effectively is crucial to the success of any podcast. By creating a schedule, prioritizing tasks, and outsourcing where necessary, you can free up more time for other commitments. It's also important to take care of yourself and avoid burnout, by maintaining a healthy work-life balance. With these tips in mind, you'll be well on your way to creating a successful podcast without sacrificing your other priorities.

CHAPTER 18: DEALING WITH CHALLENGES

Starting a podcast can be exciting, but it can also come with its fair share of challenges. In this chapter, we'll explore some common obstacles and challenges you might face when starting or running a podcast and provide you with strategies for overcoming them.

Overcoming technical difficulties

One of the most common challenges podcasters face is technical difficulties. Whether it's a faulty microphone, connection issues, or an unexpected power outage, technical difficulties can be frustrating and disruptive to your recording or publishing schedule.

To overcome technical difficulties, it's important to have backups in place. Make sure to have spare equipment on hand, such as an extra microphone, in case of equipment failure. Additionally, it's a good idea to have a backup recording in case of technical issues during a recording session. This can save a lot of time and frustration in the long run, and help you avoid missing an episode.

Handling negative feedback

Receiving negative feedback can be tough, but it's an inevitable part of being a content creator. It's important to keep in mind that not everyone will like your content, and that's okay. What's important is to listen to feedback objectively and use it to improve your content.

If you receive negative feedback, take the time to reflect on it and see if there's any truth to it. Remember that feedback is often subjective and can stem from personal preferences rather than actual issues with your content. Responding calmly and constructively to negative feedback can also help mitigate any negative impact.

Losing motivation

It's not uncommon to lose motivation when working on a long-term project like a podcast. Maybe you're not seeing the results you hoped for, or you're facing other challenges that are making it hard to stay motivated.

To overcome a lack of motivation, it's important to remind yourself of why you started your podcast in the first place. Remember the goals you set for yourself and how you felt when you first started podcasting. Revisiting your past successes and accomplishments can help reignite your motivation and inspire you to keep going.

Managing time constraints

Creating a podcast requires time, and it can be difficult to balance podcasting with other commitments. Learning time-management skills can help you better manage your schedule and overcome this challenge.

Start by creating a schedule that works for you and your other commitments. Make sure to block out specific times for podcasting so that you prioritize this work. It's also important to be realistic about your goals and schedule. If you find that you're consistently running out of time, it may be time to re-evaluate your current schedule and see what adjustments can be made.

Recovering from mistakes

Mistakes happen, and they can be especially frustrating when it comes to something as public as a podcast. However, it's important to remember that mistakes are a natural part of the learning process.

To recover from mistakes, take the time to acknowledge and reflect on what went wrong. This can help you learn from your mistakes and avoid repeating them in the future. Additionally, don't be afraid to reach out to your audience and apologize for any mistakes you've made. This can show your listeners that you take their feedback seriously and value their support.

Navigating conflicts with co-hosts or guests

Working with a co-host or guests can be a great way to share the workload and bring fresh perspectives to your podcast. However, conflicts can arise, whether it's disagreements over content or personal issues.

To navigate conflicts, it's important to communicate openly and honestly with your co-host or guests. Try to understand where they're coming from and work together to find a solution that works for everyone. If the conflict persists, it may be necessary to re-evaluate your working relationship and make changes accordingly.

Adapting to changing circumstances

The world is constantly changing, and this can impact your podcasting efforts. Whether it's changes in your personal life, changes in your niche, or changes in the industry, it's important to be able to adapt and pivot when necessary.

To adapt to changing circumstances, it's important to stay informed and keep an open mind. Keep up with industry news and trends and stay connected with your audience to understand their changing needs and preferences. Additionally, be willing to experiment and try new things to keep your podcast fresh and relevant.

Coping with fatigue and stress

Starting and running a podcast can be a lot of work, and it's not uncommon to experience fatigue and stress. It's important to take care of yourself and prioritize your mental health and well-being.

To cope with fatigue and stress, make sure to schedule time for yourself to relax and recharge. This can include taking breaks throughout the day, spending time with loved ones, or engaging in hobbies or activities you enjoy. Additionally, try to practice mindfulness and stress-reducing techniques, such as meditation, yoga, or deep breathing exercises.

In conclusion, starting and running a podcast can come with its fair share of challenges. However, by developing strategies for overcoming these obstacles and staying motivated, you can create an engaging and successful podcast that brings value to your audience and helps you achieve your goals. Remember to stay flexible, practice self-care, and keep an open mind, and you'll be on your way to podcasting success.

CHAPTER 19:
PREPARING FOR
GROWTH & SCALING

Congratulations! You have successfully launched your podcast, and now, it's time to think bigger. As your listenership grows, you will want to ensure that your podcast remains relevant and continues to deliver value to your audience. You may also want to start thinking about monetization strategies and ways to grow your podcast into a profitable business. This chapter will cover the essential steps for preparing for growth and scaling.

Developing a scalable business model

As your podcast grows, you may start to receive offers from sponsors or consider other monetization strategies. But first, you need to develop a scalable business model. Ask yourself these questions:

❖ How can you generate revenue from your podcast without compromising on content quality or the audience experience?

❖ Will the current model sustain your podcast for years to come?

❖ Can you maintain consistency while scaling up?

You may want to consider different monetization models such as sponsorships, crowdfunding, merchandising, or licensing. However, keep in mind that each model requires a different approach to managing advertising placements, marketing, and audience engagement.

Building a team to support growth

As your show gains traction, you will have more tasks to handle, such as editing, recording, marketing, and guest communication. You need to ask yourself, "What is the best use of my time?" and consider outsourcing some, if not all, of these tasks. Assembling a team can help maintain quality, consistency, and enable you to focus on strategic planning and growing your podcast.

You may want to consider hiring freelancers or part-time staff to handle specific tasks initially. However, as you scale up, you may want to consider permanent staff to take the workload off of you.

Investing in infrastructure

Technology can make or break a podcast. As you grow your podcast, you may need to upgrade your hardware and software to manage an increasing workload. You may need to switch to a higher-quality microphone, purchase editing software, or invest in equipment that helps your show grow and scale.

It is essential to research different options and consider both the upfront and long-term costs before investing. Consider purchasing products that can grow with your podcast and help you streamline your workflow.

Expanding to new markets

Once your show has established a steady listenership, it is time to think about expansion. Expanding your podcast to new markets can help you reach new audiences, build authority, and achieve growth. There are several ways to expand your podcast, including:

- ❖   Translating your podcast into different languages for international markets

- ❖   Creating new podcasts with related or different content

- ❖   Creating spinoff podcasts that focus on specific niches or aspects of your current podcast

- ❖   Introducing new segments or shows that complement your current podcast

However, before expanding, you need to ensure that you have the resources, staff, and infrastructure to handle the growing workload.

Establishing strategic partnerships

Strategic partnerships are a powerful way to elevate your podcast and gain access to new audiences. You may want to consider partnering with other podcasters, influencers, or brands that have a similar target audience. You can collaborate on new episodes, share resources, or cross-promote each other's shows, enabling you to reach a wider audience and network with other podcasters.

Developing a monetization strategy for growth

As your show gains momentum, you need to consider revenue opportunities beyond advertising. You can facilitate revenue growth by developing your monetization strategy or by allocating more resources to existing monetization models.

Consider premium content subscriptions, merchandise, affiliate partnerships, or licensing copyrighted material. Remember, your monetization strategy should align with the value you provide to your audience.

Conducting competitive analysis

As you scale, it becomes critical to analyze your competition and find ways to differentiate your podcast effectively. Competitive analysis involves a deep understanding of your competitors' strengths and weaknesses, brand strategy, content type, tone, and the target audience.

It would be best to analyze your competitors' podcasts to identify opportunities for differentiation, such as finding gaps in the market that your competitor cannot fulfill or creating a unique value proposition that sets your show apart from the competition. Competitive analysis sets your podcast up for long-term success and proves critical in identifying opportunities that lead to sustainable growth.

Leveraging growth opportunities

As your podcast scales, it is crucial to stay open to growth opportunities. Remember, sometimes the most promising opportunity may not be the most obvious one. For instance, you may be offered an opportunity to collaborate or sponsor a different type of event that caters to your audience. Stay open to new ideas and opportunities that may emerge.

When preparing for growth, it is essential to focus on creating amazing content, developing relationships with your audience, and ensuring that your podcast delivers value at every touchpoint. With the right mindset, resources, and focus, you can create a podcast that scales and grows with you.

CHAPTER 20: CONCLUSION

Congratulations, you've reached the end of this guide on how to start your own podcast! I hope you've found it informative and helpful in your journey towards creating a successful podcast. In this final chapter, I'll summarise the key points of the book and provide some additional resources for you to continue your learning and growth as a podcaster.

Throughout this book, we've covered a lot of ground on podcasting. We've looked at the benefits of starting a podcast, how to define and plan your show, equipment and software required, how to publish and distribute your podcast, monetisation strategies, building your podcast team, measuring success, legal considerations, growing your audience, creating engaging content, networking, managing your time effectively, dealing with challenges, preparing for growth, and scaling, and so much more.

I've highlighted the importance of finding your niche, defining your brand, and creating unique content that resonates with your target audience. You've learned how to record and edit your podcast, as well as how to distribute and promote it effectively. Moreover, we've discussed various monetisation strategies and emphasised the importance of creating engaging content that attracts and retains listeners.

I hope that this guide provided you with the knowledge and tools necessary to start your own podcast and grow it into a successful venture. Whether you want to make money or simply share your expertise and insights with the world, podcasting offers a unique platform for achieving your goals.

I encourage you to take action and start your podcast today. Don't be afraid to experiment and try new things. Remember that mistakes and setbacks are inevitable, but they provide invaluable learning experiences that will help you improve your show over time.

To continue your learning journey, we've compiled a list of additional resources that can help you refine your skills and stay up-to-date on the latest trends in podcasting.

> Podcast industry blogs such as Podnews, Podcast Business Journal, and Podcaster News

> Podcasting conferences and events, such as Podcast Movement and Podfest Expo

> Online forums and communities, such as Reddit's r/podcasting and the Podcasters' Support Group on Facebook.

> Podcasting courses and workshops, such as those offered on Udemy, Skillshare, and Coursera

> Podcasting books, such as The Complete Guide to Podcasting by K. M. Weiland and Podcasting for Profit by Andrew Warner

> Free podcasting resources such as Podcasting Step by Step and Buzzsprout Podcast Playbook

I hope that you find these resources helpful in your podcasting journey. Remember to keep learning, experimenting, and having fun!

I'd like to express our gratitude to you for reading this book and taking the first step towards starting your podcast. I hope it offers you the support and encouragement you need to create a successful podcast.

Lastly, I'd like to leave you on a motivational note. Believe in yourself, your abilities, and your vision. Take action and be persistent in the face of challenges. You never know what you are capable of until you try. I wish you all the best in your podcasting journey.

Final Thoughts

Congratulations! You have reached the end of How To Start Your Own Podcast. By now, you have learned everything you need to know about starting your own podcast and taking it to the next level. From developing a concept and choosing the right equipment, to recording and editing your episodes, you are now equipped with all the skills needed to begin your journey as a successful podcaster.

Always remember that starting a podcast is not just about sharing your ideas with the world. It's also about building relationships with your listeners and creating engaging content that resonates with them. Don't be afraid to experiment with different formats, styles, and topics until you find what works best for you and your audience.

As you venture into the world of podcasting, never forget that success takes time, dedication, and hard work. Stay focused on your goals, stay consistent in publishing new episodes, and continue learning from industry experts and fellow podcasters.

Thank you for reading How To Start Your Own Podcast. Now go out there, create amazing content, build an engaged following, and make your mark in this exciting industry!

ABOUT THE AUTHOR

Ray Goodwin

Ray Goodwin, is the author behind this series of captivating books on Business Development and self improvement, and has left an indelible mark on the field. He was born and raised in the bustling city of London, where he developed a strong work ethic and an insatiable curiosity about the inner workings of successful businesses. Throughout his illustrious career, Ray leveraged his extensive knowledge and experience to help numerous companies flourish and prosper.

His keen insights and innovative strategies has earned him recognition, driving him to share his expertise with others. Ray believes in the power of sharing knowledge to elevate businesses and empower aspiring entrepreneurs.

Ray's dedication to his craft is evident in the numerous books he has authored on business development and self improvement. His writing style seamlessly blends practical advice, thought-provoking concepts, and real-life case studies, making his books invaluable resources for business professionals and novices alike. His ability to distill complex concepts into accessible language has greatly impacted the lives and careers of countless individuals.

Now retired from the corporate world, Ray and his beloved wife have settled in the idyllic English countryside. Surrounded by the beauty of nature, Ray finds inspiration for his writing and indulges in his hobbies.

Ray Goodwin's books continue to serve as enduring guides for those seeking success in the business world. With a wealth of experience and a deep understanding of the inner workings of businesses, Ray's work remains a testament to his passion for sharing knowledge and helping others flourish.

www.ingramcontent.com/pod-product-compliance
Lightning Source LLC
Chambersburg PA
CBHW062355290526
45794CB00005B/2235